PETS IN THE WILD!

GUINEA PIGS IN THE WILD!

by Grace Hansen

Cody Koala
An Imprint of Pop!
popbooksonline.com

Hello! My name is Cody Koala

This book is filled with videos, puzzles, games, and more! Scan the QR codes* while you read, or visit the website below to make this book pop.

popbooksonline.com/g-pig

*Scanning QR codes requires a web-enabled smart device with a QR code reader app and a camera.

abdobooks.com

Published by Pop!, a division of ABDO, PO Box 398166, Minneapolis, Minnesota 55439. Copyright ©2025 by Abdo Consulting Group, Inc. International copyrights reserved in all countries. No part of this book may be reproduced in any form without written permission from the publisher. Cody Koala™ is a trademark and logo of Pop!.

Printed in the United States of America, North Mankato, Minnesota.
052024
092024

THIS BOOK CONTAINS RECYCLED MATERIALS

Cover Photo: Shutterstock Images
Interior Photos: Shutterstock Images, Minden Pictures
Editor: Elizabeth Andrews
Series Designer: Laura Graphenteen; Neil Klinepier

Library of Congress Control Number: 2023947445

Publisher's Cataloging-in-Publication Data
Names: Hansen, Grace, author.
Title: Guinea Pigs in the wild! / by Grace Hansen
Description: Minneapolis, Minnesota : Pop!, 2025 | Series: Pets in the wild! | Includes online resources and index
Identifiers: ISBN 9781098246136 (lib. bdg.) | ISBN 9781098246693 (ebook)
Subjects: LCSH: Guinea pigs--Juvenile literature. | Wild animals--Juvenile literature. | Wild animals as pets--Juvenile literature. | Rodents--Juvenile literature. | Rodents--Behavior--Juvenile literature.
Classification: DDC 636.0887--dc23

Table of Contents

Chapter 1
Guinea Pigs 4

Chapter 2
Guinea Pigs in the Wild . . . 8

Chapter 3
Pet Guinea Pigs 14

Chapter 4
Caring for Guinea Pigs 16

Making Connections 22
Glossary 23
Index 24
Online Resources 24

Chapter 1

Guinea Pigs

Guinea pigs are **rodents**. Their name traces back to England in the 1600s. They were sold for one **guinea** each. Some people believe the word "pig" comes from their small and sturdy bodies.

Guinea pigs are **herbivores**. In the wild, their diet is mainly made up of seeds, twigs, grasses, and hay. Their teeth help them nibble, grind, and chew food.

Chapter 2

Guinea Pigs in the Wild

Guinea pigs are from South America. They can be found from Venezuela to Argentina. They live in many different **habitats**, including swamps, grasslands, and forest edges.

Where Some Wild Guinea Pigs Live

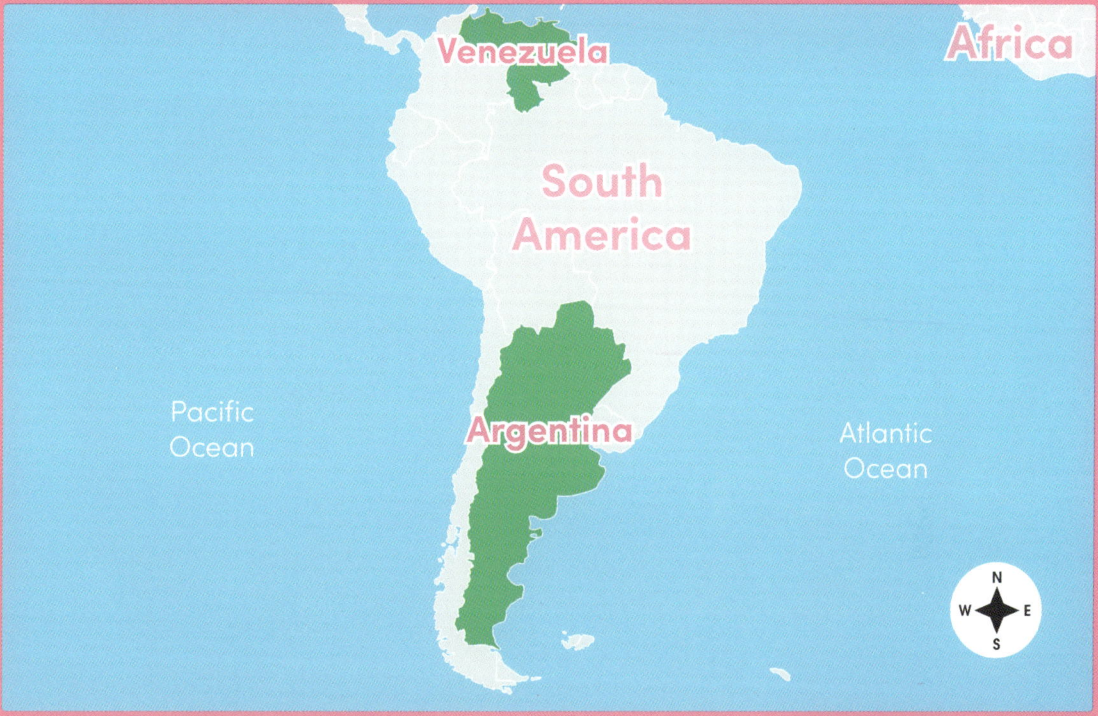

Venezuela

Africa

South America

Pacific Ocean

Argentina

Atlantic Ocean

Learn more here!

Guinea pigs find shelter wherever they can. Some use **burrows** of other animals to hide in. When they are not resting, they search for food.

Guinea pigs are social creatures. They live in small family groups. They feed together and **groom** one another. They communicate using many different noises.

Guinea pigs chirp, purr, squeal, and grunt.

Chapter 3

Pet Guinea Pigs

The most common type of pet guinea pig is *Cavia porcellus*. It does not live in the wild. However, it is closely related to some wild guinea pigs.

Explore links here!

Chapter 4

Caring for Guinea Pigs

Guinea pigs are social creatures. **Ideally**, a person would own more than one guinea pig. In any case, guinea pigs should have lots of daily interaction with their owners.

Guinea pigs are active for about 20 hours a day.

Complete an activity here!

Guinea pigs need the largest **habitat** possible. The habitat should have at least one to two inches (2.5–5.1cm)

of bedding and a hide box for each animal. It should also be escape proof.

Guinea pigs should be fed high-quality food. They also need fresh, clean water daily. Guinea pigs that are loved and cared for can live up to eight years.

Making Connections

Text-to-Self

What do you like best about guinea pigs?

Text-to-Text

Have you read any other books about guinea pigs? What did you learn in those books that was not in this one?

Text-to-World

Can you think of any other animals that live in South America? How are they similar to and different from a guinea pig?

Glossary

burrow – a hole that an animal digs in the ground for shelter.

groom – to clean the coat or fur of an animal.

guinea – a coin minted in Great Britain between 1663 and 1814.

habitat – the natural environment of an animal; a safe space for a pet animal to live.

herbivore – an animal that only eats plants.

ideally – for best results.

rodent – any of several related animals that have large front teeth for chewing. Common rodents include mice, squirrels, and beavers.

Index

burrow, 11
care, 16, 18, 21
Cavia porcellus, 14
England, 4
food, 7, 11, 21

habitat, 8, 11, 18
habits, 11–12, 16
life span, 21
South America, 8
teeth, 7

Online Resources

popbooksonline.com

Thanks for reading this **Cody Koala book!**

This book is filled with videos, puzzles, games, and more! Scan the QR codes* while you read, or visit the website below to make this book pop.

popbooksonline.com/g-pig

*Scanning QR codes requires a web-enabled smart device with a QR code reader app and a camera.